# What happens?

By Christopher Phillips

What happens when you live life to the fullest?

What happens when
you live life to the dullest?

What happens when you feel no one cares?

What happens when
you feel lighter than air?

What happens when
you play with abandon?

What happens when
your kindness is random?

What happens when you arrive late?

What happens when you hesitate?

What happens when
you romp in the rain?

What happens when you feel someone's pain?

What happens when you right a wrong?

What happens when you make up a song?

What happens when you have lots of luck?

# What happens when you feel like you're stuck?

What happens when
you give someone a flower?

What happens when
you do not know the hour?

What happens when you're afraid to feel?

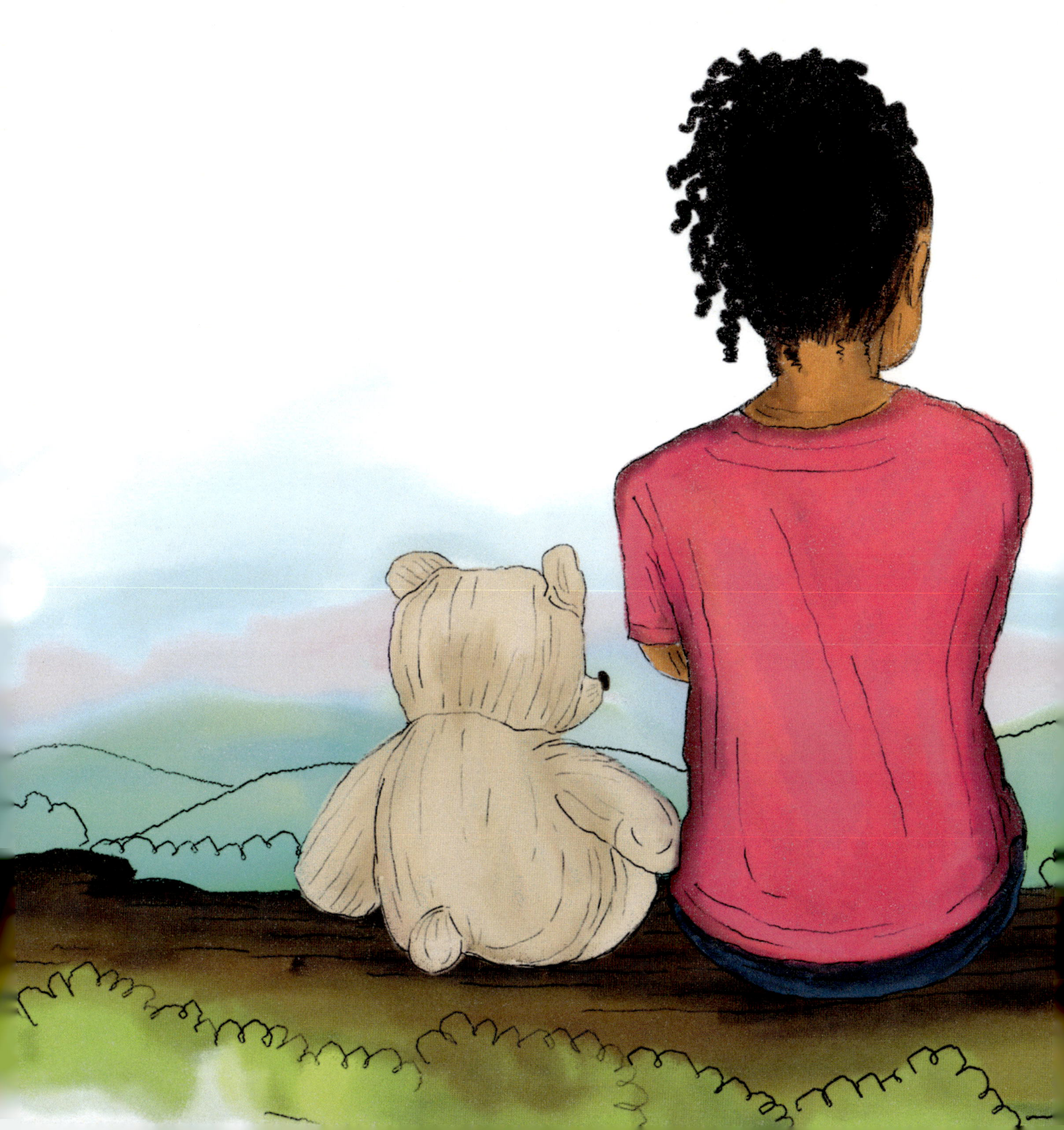

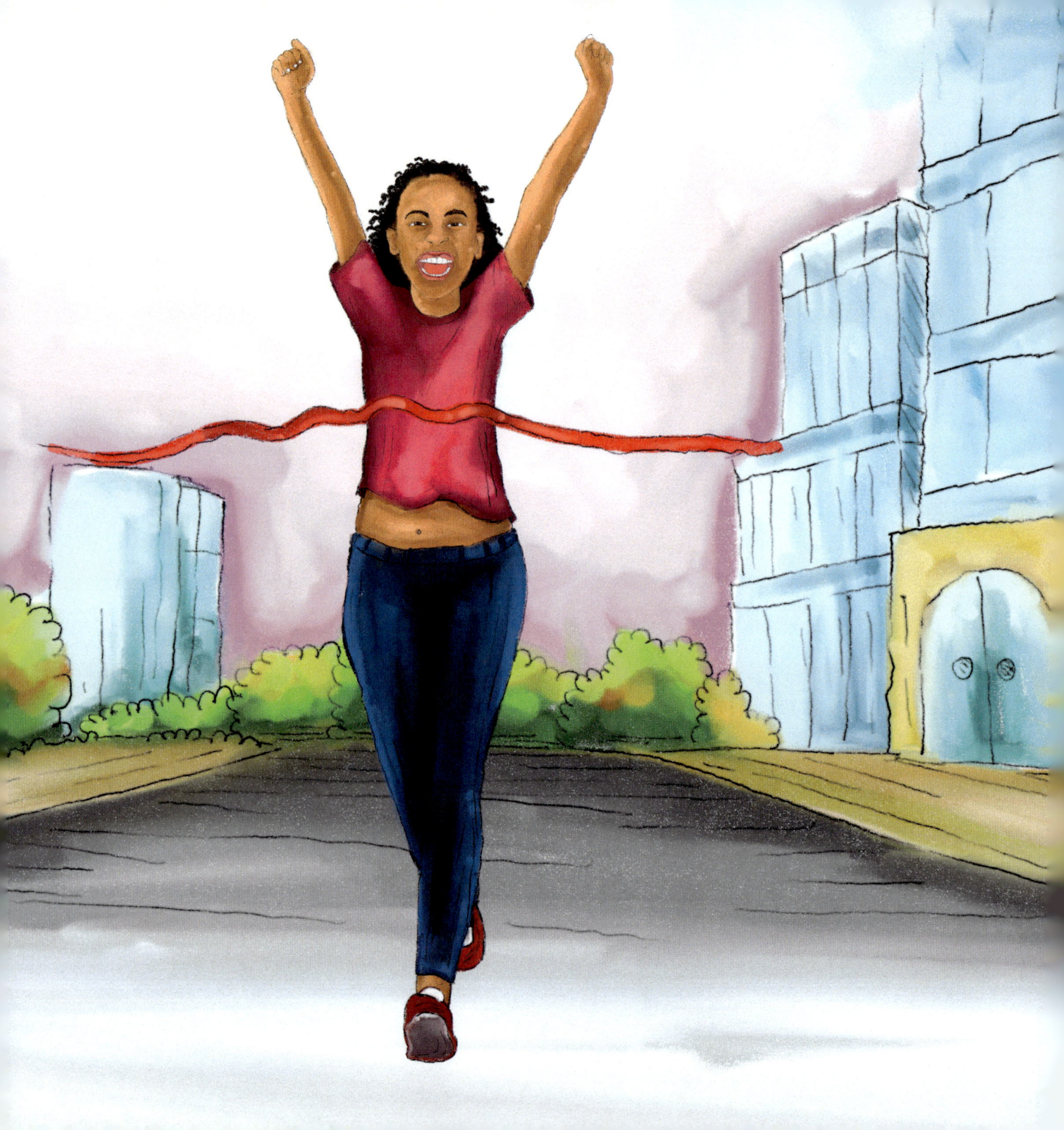

What happens when you're ready to heal?

What happens when
you go round and round?

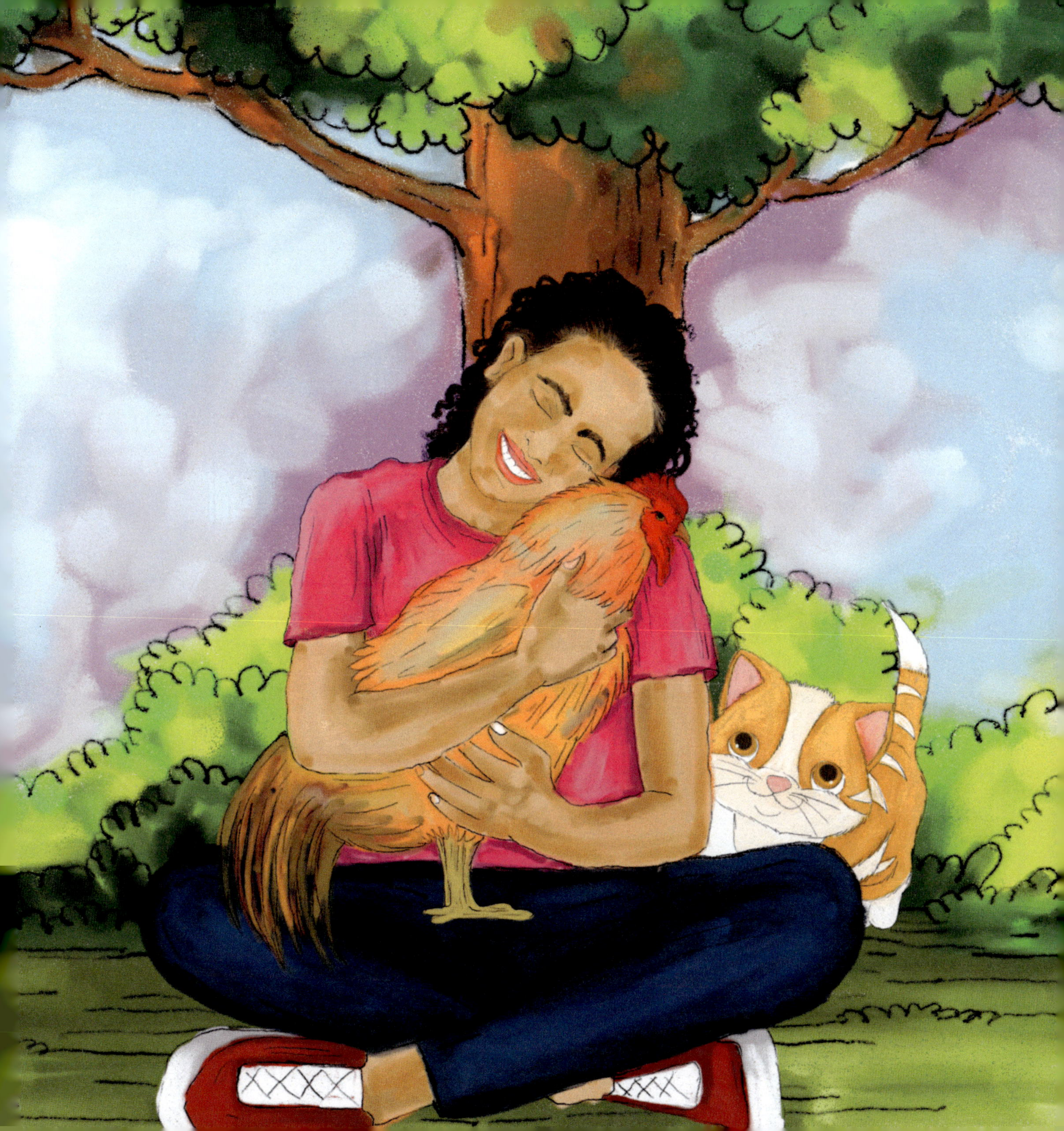

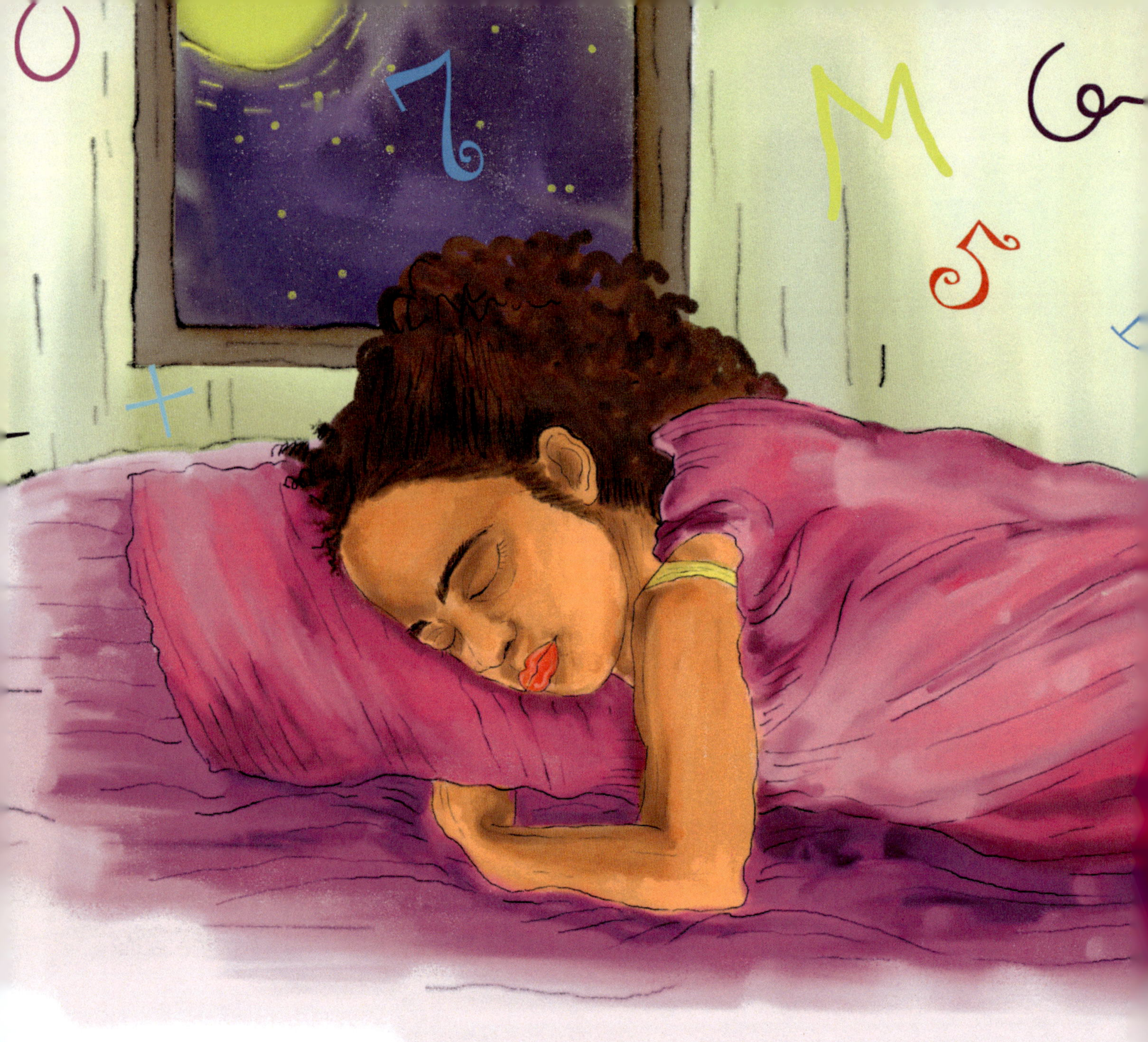

What happens when
it's time to lie down?

**Written by**
Christopher Phillips

**Illustrations by**
Arabage N. Priyadarshani

**Editorial design by**
Ene de julieta

Made in the USA
Columbia, SC
28 June 2023